D1469847

Language
Network

McDougal Littell
A HOUGHTON MIFFLIN COMPANY
Evanston, Illinois • Boston • Dallas

ISBN 0-618-05273-9

3 4 5 6 7 8 9 – RRW – 04 03 02 01 00

Contents

Chapter 4: Process Assessment: Observing Students in Progress 39

Copymasters

Chapter 5: Portfolio Assessment: Compiling a Collection 53

Copymasters

Chapter One

Introduction to Assessment

Not too long ago, the word *assessment* conjured up a single image in many people's minds: rows of students, sitting quietly, responding to questions on written tests. Today the word *assessment* creates many different images and raises just as many questions:

- What should I be assessing?

- What are the kinds of assessments?

- What is the most comprehensive way to assess my students?

- How can I prepare my students for assessment?

What is happening in the world of assessment? For as long as anyone can remember, formal assessments, primarily paper-and-pencil tests, have been the most popular way to measure a student's progress in school. Their popularity stems from their ease of use and their application as an objective measuring instrument. They are based on the belief that the knowledge a student has acquired is the most accurate indication of his or her ability.

Over time educators have begun to want more information about their students than could be gleaned from formal assessment and, as a result, have sought ways to get a broader view of their students' skills and abilities. They want assessment to mirror what they see from their students every day in the classroom. Many have turned to alternative assessments that involve students in complex, multimodal activities. These assessments help teachers see their students holistically as critical thinkers, problem solvers, and acquirers of knowledge.

Although often seen as opposing methods, formal and alternative assessments are not necessarily in conflict. They are different ways of measuring student performance, with different goals and outcomes. A complete assessment program includes both formal and alternative assessments; a complete student profile includes results from both kinds of instruments.

The diagrams on the next two pages offer a more complete description of formal and alternative assessment.

FORMAL ASSESSMENT

Four types of formal assessment instruments are commonly used.

Standardized Tests
- measure a student's performance in various skill areas against students in other districts or across the country
- compare results with national norms
  - ✳ example: nationally published standardized tests given once a year

Criterion-Referenced Tests
- measure whether a student has attained mastery of an instructional objective
- compare results with set percentage
  - ✳ example: classroom, school, or district tests that measure a specified instructional objective

FORMAL ASSESSMENT

**Program Tests
Teacher-Made Tests**
- measure retention and comprehension of specific content
  - ✳ example: selection and Part Tests for *The Language of Literature*

Essay Tests
- measure ability of student to express self in writing, given a prompt or specific assignment
- measure some content knowledge
  - ✳ example: state writing tests

Characteristics of Formal Assessment

1. Formal assessment asks the question: **What do you know?** The primary purpose is to measure the knowledge a student has acquired from what has been taught.

2. The emphasis is on recall, generally via paper and pencil tests. The tests usually include matching, true-false, and multiple-choice items.

3. The tests are usually on demand, meaning students are given a specific time frame in which to perform.

4. Formal assessment allows for different kinds of comparisons. In standardized tests, results are compared with national norms; in criterion-referenced tests, results are compared with a set percentage. With these tests, a student's performance can be compared with that of other students in the classroom, district, or country.

ALTERNATIVE ASSESSMENT

Alternative assessment is sometimes called authentic assessment or performance-based assessment. The web below shows techniques and instruments associated with alternative assessment.

Product and Performance Assessment
- requires students to produce a tangible product or create a performance that demonstrates their understanding of skills and concepts
- focuses teacher's attention on the final results rather than the processes, behaviors, or strategies students used to create them
- is based on judgment guided by criteria
  * examples: essay, speech, model

Process Assessment
- requires students to demonstrate or share their processes, behaviors, strategies, and critical thinking abilities as they work to understand skills and concepts
- focuses teacher's attention on student processes, behaviors, and strategies rather than the final results
- is based on judgment guided by criteria
  * example: reading strategies, writing drafts

ALTERNATIVE ASSESSMENT

Portfolio Assessment
- a purposeful collection of student work that exhibits the student's overall efforts, progress, and achievements over time in one or more areas of the curriculum

Characteristics of Alternative Assessment

1. Alternative assessment asks the questions: **What can you do?** and **How do you do it?** The primary purpose is to get a broad picture of a student as critical thinker, problem solver, and acquirer of knowledge.

2. Tasks and experiences used for assessment are already familiar to students and include the rich variety found in most classrooms, including projects, products, simulations, and other examples of a student's own work.

3. Assessment is ongoing. Rather than being limited to on-demand, single-event tests, students have the opportunity to show what they can do in a variety of tasks over time.

4. Both teacher and student are actively involved in the assessment process. Reflection, self-assessment, observation, and participation are at the heart of alternative assessment.

5. Because authentic assessment is holistic, teachers often engage in many of the assessment practices described above for a single task or experience.

Assessment Options in *Language Network*

TEACHER'S RESOURCES

Assessment Masters booklet:

Chapter Tests
- **Pretests** Assess students' knowledge before starting each chapter.
- **Mid-point Tests** Check students' progress midway through each chapter.
- **Mastery Tests** Assess students' knowledge after they complete each chapter.

Grammar, Usage, and Mechanics Mastery Tests
These tests include passages of text followed by multiple-choice questions that ask students to identify errors in sentence construction, English usage, spelling, capitalization, and punctuation. The tests also gauge students' knowledge of grammar terminology and grammatical structures.

Writing Prompts, Rubrics, and Student Models
- **Writing Prompts** These writing assignments correspond to the Writing Workshops. Additional writing prompts can be found at mcdougallittell.com.
- **Rubrics** Use these rubrics to help you evaluate and assess students' writing.
- **Student Models** Strong, average, and weak annotated student models give students insights into the assessment process.

Test Preparation booklet (*College Test Preparation* for Grades 11–12):
Test-taking strategies and instruction are followed by practice questions to help students prepare for tests such as the *ITBS (Iowa Tests of Basic Skills)*, *Stanford Achievement Test Series*, *TerraNova*, SAT and ACT.

Daily Test Preparation transparencies:
Use these transparencies to give students quick daily lessons in test preparation. Teaching tips are included for each lesson.

Students Acquiring English/ESL Test Preparation booklet:
This booklet provides test tips and strategies specifically geared toward students acquiring English.

Online Test Preparation at mcdougallittell.com:
Timed practice tests with automatic scoring give students another option for test preparation.

PUPIL'S EDITION:

Diagnostic Tests appear before each grammar chapter.

Exercise Bank allows assessment of lesson mastery.

Mastery Tests follow each grammar chapter.

Writing Workshops provide opportunities to assess student writing.

Portfolio Building opportunities are provided in each chapter.

Planning Your Assessment Program

Teacher's Guide to Assessment and Portfolio Use has been prepared for those teachers who want to expand their knowledge and use of a wide variety of assessment practices. Each chapter describes steps that you can take to use the range of options available to you and develop a comprehensive picture of your students as complex learners.

Chapter Two

Getting Started

What makes assessment effective? Most educators would give a one-word answer: authenticity. Authentic assessment has two components—an authentic assessment task and an interactive means of evaluating it.

Understanding Authentic Assessment   An authentic assessment task is a task that comes close to what you want the student to be able to do.

- If you want to know how well students can read and understand literature, assess them with complete, unedited literature selections, not contrived paragraphs created especially for the assessment.

- If you want to evaluate students as complex thinkers and problem solvers, assess them with complex multimodal activities.

- If you want to understand students' behaviors, strategies, and processes, assess them through observation and discussion in the context of classroom and real-world experiences.

When you use authentic tasks for assessment, students will easily see the connection between what they're learning and what they're expected to know, because the two are synonymous.

Involving Your Students   Customarily the responsibility for evaluation has been the teacher's. However, since it is the student who is doing the learning, authentic assessment requires that both teacher and student actively participate in the process. The more students know about how they learn, the more they'll be able to take responsibility for their own learning. This skill will help bridge the gap between the classroom and the world outside of school, enabling them to become lifelong learners.

Incorporating the following suggestions into your classroom practices will help you help your students begin to take charge of their own learning.

Finding Out Where You Are

Taking a close look at your current assessment practices will help you understand how you are spending your assessment time and give you an opportunity to consider adjustments you would like to make. Use teacher inventory copymasters on pages 8–10 to conduct your own self-assessment: *Teacher Inventory: Assessment Practices and Interests* on page 8 will help you examine the assessments you are currently using. *Teacher Inventory: Assessment Tools* on page 9 provides a format for you to analyze why and when you use various assessment instruments. *Teacher Inventory: Classroom Practices* on page 10 will help you examine your assessment practices and get started making some adjustments.

Establishing an Effective Environment

If self-assessment is to be useful, students must be willing to honestly report their ideas, beliefs, intentions, and thinking processes. For this to happen , students must believe they will be heard and respected. You can help establish this belief during the first week of school by introducing self-assessment as an integral past of the assessment process.

At the beginning of the school year, ask your students to write a letter describing themselves as readers, writers, and classroom participants. Have them describe what they hope to accomplish in the coming year. Or, if you prefer, have them complete **Student Self-Assessment: Reading** and **Student Self-Assessment: Writing** on pages 11–14. Have them keep their inventories in their notebooks.

Encourage them to revisit their letter or retake the self-assessment inventories several times during the year, noting what has changed.

Incorporating Assessment Practices Throughout the Year

Once students understand that they will be actively involved in the learning processes, make sure that you provide activities and vehicles that will reinforce this approach. Following are some useful strategies that will help you accomplish this goal.

1. **Help students set goals.**
   In order to grow as learners, students must become actively involved in setting goals for themselves. Their goals can be for a day, a week, a project, or the year. Whatever the duration, encourage students to consider their strengths and limitations so that the goals they set will be realistic. Sample copymasters, called **Goal-Setting**, are provided on pages 15 and 16. You can help your students by meeting with them periodically about their goals. **Student-Teacher Conference Form** on page 17 provides an outline for your meeting.

2. **Introduce student contracts.**
   An effective student contract provides an outline and timetable for a task or project. By concretely defining students' responsibilities, a contract can help students meet these responsibilities. Meet with students periodically to gauge their performance in terms of their contract. Two different samples, called **Student Contract**, are provided on pages 18–19. Use one or both to help students commit themselves to their work.

3. **Help students get into the habit of reflecting on what they're doing and how well they're doing it.**
   This is one of the most effective ways for students to learn. Reflecting can also help students take risks, because they realize that they are in charge of their learning and that it is an ongoing process.

4. Encourage peer review as a regular part of the assessment process.
Peer review will help students understand that their audience isn't just you; it includes everyone who reads or sees what they produce.

5. Help your students learn to operate independently of you.
Be a coach. Observe and offer suggestions. Provide guided opportunities for them to use new learning strategies. Structure opportunities for collaboration. Through activities like these, you can be a mentor to your students and help them become independent.

Support for an Effective Environment in *Language Network*

Language Network provides many opportunities for establishing an environment for effective assessment.

- Students can check their work in the SELF-CHECKS provided for all grammar lessons.

- The Student Help Desk ending every chapter contains a checklist of the skills presented in that chapter.

- Each Writing Workshop incorporates reflection and peer review as an integral part of the writing process. Students receive additional support from Peer Response Guide Sheets in *Writing and Communication Masters.*

- Portfolio references in each chapter help students see the many opportunities they have to build their collection.

- *Teacher's Guide to Assessment and Portfolio* Use provides ideas and copymasters to help you establish an effective environment.

Teacher Inventory:
Assessment Practices and Interests

1. What percentage of classroom time do you spend on assessment activities?

1%	3%
5%	10%

2. Of your assessment time, what percentage do you spend in each of the following categories?

	25%	50%	75%	100%
A. Formal Assessment				
Standardized Tests				
Criterion-Referenced Tests				
Program Tests				
Teacher-Made Tests				
B. Alternative Assessment				
Product and Performance Assessment				
Process Assessment				
Portfolio Assessment				

3. Of the kinds of assessments you use, which do you prefer?

_____

Why? _____

4. Of the assessments you use, which do you have the most confidence in?

_____

Why? _____

5. Of the assessments you have read about which would you like to learn

more about? _____

Why? _____

Teacher Inventory: Assessment Tools

Directions: Use this form to develop your own list of the assessment tools you now use. Consider tools such as classroom quizzes, program tests, portfolios and other vehicles you use to assess students. When you're finished, evaluate your practices for adjustments you would like to make.

Assessment Tools	Reason for Use	When Used

Teacher Inventory: Classroom Practices

1. Check the practices listed below you are currently using.

    _____ A. Variety of tasks in the classroom and for assessment

    _____ B. Student self-assessment

    _____ C. Goal setting

    _____ D. Student contracts

    _____ E. Reflecting

    _____ F. Peer review

    _____ G. Working toward student independence

    _____ H. Interviewing

    _____ I. Observation

2. Of the practices you use, which do you find to be the most successful?

    Why? _____

    _____

    _____

3. Which of the practices listed above would you like to add to your repertoire?

    _____

    _____

    Why? _____

4. How might you incorporate this practice? What actions might you take?

    _____

    _____

    _____

Student Self-Assessment: Reading

Directions: Use this form to describe your attitude and thoughts toward reading at this time. You may circle more than one answer on any item.

1. These are my thoughts and attitude about reading:
   a. I like to read, both at home and at school.
   b. I like to read for fun, but not for school.
   c. I really don't like to read and would rather do other things.
   d. I would like to read more if I were a better reader.
   e. I would like to read more if I had more time.
   f. I like to read aloud.
   g. I do not like to read aloud.

2. These are my thoughts and attitude about reading at home:
   a. It's a waste of time.
   b. It helps me escape and relax.
   c. I only read when I have to for an assignment.
   d. I read mostly for entertainment.
   e. I read mostly for information.
   f. I love to read and wish I had more time for it.

3. I consider myself to be
   a. a very good reader.
   b. a good reader.
   c. an average reader.
   d. a poor reader.

4. In order to read and understand material for school,
   a. I read best when I'm alone in a quiet place.
   b. I read best with things going on around me.
   c. I read best aloud with another student or in a small group.
   d. I read best when the teacher tells us what to look for first.
   e. I understand more when I have a long period of time to read.
   f. I understand more when I read in short little spurts.
   g. I read the material twice.

5. These problems bother me when I am reading:
   a. There are too many words that I don't know.
   b. I read too slowly.
   c. I read too fast and forget things.
   d. I get bored quickly and stop paying attention.
   e. My eyes get tired easily.
   f. Other things distract me.

For the following questions, choose the answer that fits your habits *most* of the time.

6. How often do you read each of the following? Circle your answer.

a. newspapers	never	sometimes	often	usually
b. magazines	never	sometimes	often	usually
c. novels	never	sometimes	often	usually
d. comic books	never	sometimes	often	usually
e. books of information	never	sometimes	often	usually

7. How much time do you spend at home reading for enjoyment?
   a. never
   b. up to 30 minutes a week
   c. 30 to 60 minutes a week
   d. more than an hour a week
   e. an hour a day or more

8. Circle the topics or types of literature you like to read.
   a. young adult novels   i. fantasy
   b. adventure/survival   j. myths and legends
   c. science fiction   k. science
   d. mysteries   l. poetry
   e. sports   m. biographies
   f. stories about animals   n. history
   g. humorous stories   o. travel/other places
   h. historical fiction   p. news articles

9. What is the best book you have ever read?

   _____

10. What is the best book you have read lately?

   _____

11. Look at the scale below and put an X where you think you belong.

I am not good at reading.		I am OK at reading.		I am good at reading.

1	2	3	4	5	6	7	8	9	10

Student Self-Assessment: Writing

Directions: Use this form to describe your thoughts and attitude toward writing at this time. You may circle more than one answer on any item.

1. These are my thoughts and attitude toward writing:
   a. I like to write, both at home and at school.
   b. I like to write for fun, but not for school.
   c. I really don't like to write and would rather do other things.
   d. I don't think writing is a very useful tool for everyday living.
   e. I would like to write more if I were a better writer.
   f. I would like to write more if I had more time.

2. I spend this amount of time at home writing for enjoyment:
   a. no time
   b. up to 30 minutes a week
   c. 30–60 minutes a week
   d. more than an hour a week
   e. an hour a day or more

3. I consider myself to be
   a. a very good writer.
   b. a good writer.
   c. an average writer.
   d. a poor writer.

4. This is how I would describe my improvement as a writer:
   a. I feel as though I am improving as a writer.
   b. I know what I need to work on as a writer.
   c. I am not improving as a writer.
   d. I don't know what to work on to improve my writing.

5. These problems bother me when I am writing:
   a. I have trouble thinking of topics to write about.
   b. I have trouble expressing my ideas.
   c. I have trouble thinking of just the right word.
   d. I have trouble organizing my ideas.
   e. I have trouble getting started.
   f. Other things distract me.

6. When I am working on a writing project
   a. I would rather work alone than with a group.
   b. I would rather work with one other person.
   c. I would rather work with a group.
   d. I don't care whether I work with alone or with a group.

7. I prefer to have my writing reviewed by
   a. a peer reader.
   b. a small group of peer readers.
   c. a peer reader and my teacher.
   d. my teacher only.
   e. no one.

8. I most like to write
   a. in a diary or journal.
   b. letters to friends.
   c. stories or mysteries.
   d. poems.
   e. about my opinions.
   f. directions that tell others how to do something.
   g. about my life.
   i. about other people.
   j. about inventions and ideas.
   k. about the news at school.

   l. _____

9. In my free time I like to write
   a. cartoons.
   b. song lyrics.
   c. notes to friends.
   d. a diary or a journal.
   e. plays.
   f. computer notes.
   g. letters.
   h. jokes and puzzles.

   i. _____

10. The best piece of writing I have done is _____
_____

I like this about it. _____
_____

11. Look at the scale below and put an X where you belong.

I am not good at writing.				I am OK at writing.				I am good at writing.	
1	2	3	4	5	6	7	8	9	10

Goal Setting

Directions: Use this form to help you set and achieve one goal for yourself. You may focus your ideas in one area, like writing, or be more general. If you choose, add the completed form to your portfolio and review it one month later. Evaluate how well you achieved your goal.

Things I Can Do Now

_____

_____

_____

_____

_____

_____

Things I Need to Work On

_____

_____

_____

_____

_____

_____

One Goal I Have for Myself Is

_____

_____

_____

_____

_____

_____

I'll Know When I've Reached That Goal When

_____

_____

_____

_____

_____

_____

_____

Goal Setting

Directions: Use this form to help you set one goal for yourself and to think about how others can help you meet it.

1. This is what I am trying to do.

   _____

   _____

2. This is my attitude toward it.

   _____

   _____

3. This is how my classmates can help me.

   _____

   _____

4. This is how my teacher can help me.

   _____

   _____

5. This is how my family and friends can help me.

   _____

   _____

   Signed _____

   _____

Follow-up: This is what happened.

_____

_____

_____

_____

_____

_____

Goal Setting: Student-Teacher Conference Form

Directions: Use this form to discuss goals with students.

1. What goals have you set for yourself since our last meeting?

2. In your opinion, how well have you met these goals?

3. How has meeting these goals helped you in school?

4. What two or three new goals do you want to work toward?

Teacher Comments

Student Contract

Directions: Complete this form before you begin working on your assignment or project.

On this day, _____, I,_____, do hereby agree to complete the following tasks to the best of my ability.

Required Assignments

A.

B.

C.

Optional Assignments

D.

E.

F.

To demonstrate what I have learned, I will do the following:

I will stay on task in class, working alone or with others. I understand that work not completed during class time must be done at home. The rules for this contract have been explained, and I understand them.

Student Signature_____

I will provide help when necessary and respond to work quickly.

Teacher Signature_____

Student Contract

Directions: Complete this form before you begin working on your assignment or project.

1. I will be starting my work on _____

   I will complete my work by _____

2. What I want to find out:

3. Resources I will need:

4. Places I will look for information:

5. Some problems I expect to encounter:

6. How I will share my findings:

7. Who will evaluate my work:

8. The criteria that will be used to evaluate my work:

9. The grade, score, or comments I will work toward:

Student Signature _____

Teacher Signature _____

Chapter Three

Product and Performance Assessment: Looking at Final Results

In product and performance assessment, the student is required to produce a tangible product or develop a performance as evidence that knowledge has been gained and a goal has been met. Because products and performance have long been a popular component of many classrooms, this assessment is relatively easy to add to your repertoire. Look over the examples on this page and note how many you are already doing in your classes.

Characteristics of Product and Performance Assessment

1. Product and performance assessment places more emphasis on the final results than it does on the process used in getting there. As an evaluator, you should make every effort to keep the process used separate from the final results. Process shouldn't be ignored, but it shouldn't be a factor in your evaluation of the end result.

2. Products or performance can be short-term or long-term, taking a class period, several days or weeks, or even several months to complete. In some districts or states, a major project is a graduation requirement. In those situations, the student might take the entire school year to complete the project.

3. Students can do projects alone or in groups.

4. Product and performances are often multi-part, involving several stages, components, and tasks. For that reason, the final result is apt to be as successful as the planning and organizing that the student puts into it. Students learn to manage their time and effort in doing a number of products or projects.

Examples of Products and Performances

advertisement	costume	jewelry	petition	scenery for a play
architectural	crafts	joke/riddle	photo album	scrapbook
design	dance	kites	picture	script
audiotape	debate	maps	dictionary	scroll
autobiography	diorama	memoir	piñata	sculpture
award	directory	menu	poem	shadow box
biography	editorial	mobile	pop-up book	short story
brochure	essay	mock trial	post card	skit
bulletin board	eulogy	mosaic	poster	slide show
chart	fable	mural	puppets/puppet	song/song lyrics
children's book	family tree	museum	show	speech
collage	fashion show	musical	questionnaire	survey
collection	fiction	instrument	rap	talent show
comic strip	flag	needlework	recipe	terrarium
computer	flip chart	news story	recital	time capsule
program	flow chart	oral history	research	time line
constitution	games/puzzles	painting/drawing	paper/report	videotape
contract	graph	pamphlet	review/books,	
cooking demo	interview	panel discussion	movies	
correspondence	invention	pantomime	scale model	

Ensuring Success

For some students, projects are an enjoyable alternative. For others, the less structured format may be stressful. You can help ensure success by providing guidance during the planning stages.

1. **Provide students with a list of optional performances and product formats.**
   Try to give enough different options so students can find products that match their preferred learning modes. Refer to the list on this page for ideas.

2. **Introduce proposals as a way for students to get focused.**
   A sample format, *Proposal,* is provided on page 23.

3. **Have students prepare action plans and task sheets.**
   By looking at the whole process before they begin a project, students will make better decisions about how to proceed whether they are working alone or in a group. Copymasters, called *Action Plan* and *Task Sheet*, on pages 24–26 provide three different ways for students to organize their work.

4. **Have students determine how they want to work.**
   If you try product assessment more than once, have students work alone sometimes and in groups sometimes.

Assessing Progress

When using products and performances for assessments purposes, be sure you have appropriate evaluation instruments. The following examples may help you.

1. **Require periodic progress reports.**
   Sample formats on pages 27–28 provide different ideas for reporting progress. If you want students to use compatible formats to plan their work and report their progress, use *Progress Report* on page 27 in conjunction with *Task Sheet* on page 26. *Mini-Progress Report* on page 28 provides a format for reporting daily progress.

2. **Establish criteria for a successful product or performance through rubrics and other devices.**
   You can use the copymasters on pages 29–33 as ready-made rubrics: *Holistic Guide: Writing; Holistic Guide: Oral Presentation; Rubric: Oral Presentation;* and *Rubric Product / Performance*. If you want to develop criteria with your students at the beginning of the project, use the scoring templates on pages 34 and 36.

3. **Incorporate peer review as part of the assessment process.**
   A sample format, *Peer Assessment*, on page 35 will give you ideas for ways to involve your students in peer review. The basic criteria outline on this copymaster is the same as found on pages 33 and 34 (see above).

4. **Include self-assessment at every stage of the assessment process.**
   Encourage your students to reflect on their learning styles, habits, and strengths. Sample formats, *Self-Assessment: Products/Performance*, on pages 37–38 provide students with ways to think about their experiences.

Support for Product and Performance Assessment in *Language Network*

Language Network includes many ideas for products, projects, and performances throughout the program.

- Writing Workshops and chapters about the media suggest many ways students can incorporate their writing into a larger project.

- Oral communication chapters and features such as Speak for Yourself and Grammar Across the Curriculum provide many product and performance ideas.

- *Teacher's Guide to Assessment and Portfolio Use* contains many helpful suggestions and copymasters that will help you with product and performance assessment.

Proposal

Directions: Use this form to help clarify your thinking about your product or performance.

1. Topic: _____

2. What do you expect to discover or communicate?

   _____
   _____
   _____
   _____
   _____

3. How do you wish to work?

   Alone: _____

   Work with: _____

4. How do you propose to demonstrate what you've learned?

   _____
   _____
   _____
   _____
   _____

5. What materials or technology will you need to present what you've learned?

   _____
   _____
   _____
   _____
   _____

Action Plan

Directions: Use this form to think through and organize your work.

1. I will choose a topic that meets the following requirements:

   _____

   _____

   _____

2. I will choose the formats for my presentation from among these options:

   _____ audiotape/videotape   _____ series of photographs

   _____ filmstrip   _____ essay

   _____ slides   _____ other _____

3. I will narrow the focus of my topic and then conduct research.

4. I will keep a record of my sources.

   _____ use print resources

   _____ conduct interviews

   _____ use technology

   _____ use at least _____different sources

5. I will organize my content so I have clear main ideas. I will discuss this with my teacher.

6. I will use the following methods to plan my product.

   _____ storyboard

   _____ outline

   _____ flow chart

   _____ action plan

   _____ other _____

7. I will finish the product by

   _____ editing my material

   _____ proofreading my script

   _____ giving my product a title

   _____ giving my product an introduction and conclusion

Task Sheet

Directions: Use this form to organize your work. List the tasks you need to complete, the target date, person responsible, and necessary materials.

Task	Target Date	Person Responsible	Materials Needed

Task Sheet

Directions: Use this form to organize your work and time. Review the steps outlined in the left-hand column below. List the tasks that need to be completed under each heading. Then decide who is responsible for each task and when it needs to be completed.

Steps and Tasks	Completed by Whom	By When
Planning		
Research		
Development		
Exhibition or Presentation of Product		

Progress Report

Directions: Use this form to report your progress. List the tasks that need to be completed under each heading. Then describe how your project is progressing.

Steps and Tasks	Progress
Planning	
Research	
Development	
Exhibition or Presentation of Product	

Mini-Progress Report

Directions: Complete this progress report by describing work you finished today and what you plan to do tomorrow.

Today I spent _____ minutes investigating this topic:	I learned some new ideas about the topic. They are:
Today I completed:	Tomorrow I plan to:

Holistic Guide: Writing

The following holistic guide shows the features that tend to appear in a range of student papers representing various levels of accomplishment. The aim of the guide is to help you evaluate student papers according to a set of standards. A single student's paper may not include all the characteristics identified with any one score point, but it can be assigned a score by looking for the description that most nearly matches its features or its dominant impression. Some allowance should be made for minor errors in style, usage, mechanics, and spelling on the unit assessment, since that test does not provide time for revision.

Level: Strong

Exceptional 6 points	Commendable 5 points
A paper at score point 6 • has a clear and consistent focus. • has a logical organization. • uses transitions to connect ideas. • supports ideas with details, quotations, examples, and/or other evidence. • exhibits well-formed sentences varying in structure. • exhibits a rich vocabulary, including precise language that is appropriate for the purpose and audience of the paper. • contains almost no errors in usage, mechanics, and spelling.	A paper at score point 5 has the same general features of organization and effective elaboration as a 6-point paper, but it represents a somewhat less accomplished performance. It may, for example, • have an organization that is predictable or unnecessarily mechanical. • lack the depth and logical precision of a 6-point paper in presenting its argument and supporting evidence. • exhibit appropriate sentence variety and vocabulary but without the control and richness of a 6-point paper. • contain a few errors in usage, mechanics, and spelling.

Level: Average

Proficient	4 points	Basic	3 points

A paper at score point 4

- has a fairly clear focus that may occasionally become obscured.

- shows an organizational pattern, but relationships between ideas may sometimes be difficult to understand.

- contains supporting evidence that may lack effect and so only superficially develops ideas.

- has complete and varied sentences most of the time.

- contains some errors in usage, mechanics, and spelling but which do not confuse meaning.

A paper at score point 3

- has a vague focus and so may contain irrelevant details or digressions.

- shows an attempt at organization, but connections between ideas are difficult to understand.

- lacks important supporting evidence, or the evidence cited does not sufficiently develop ideas.

- shows little sentence variety.

- contains several serious errors in usage, mechanics, and spelling which cause distraction and some confusion about meaning.

Level: Weak

Limited	2 points	Minimal	1 point

A paper at score point 2

- has a topic but does not include any elaboration.

- lacks plausible support for ideas.

- shows limited word choice.

- contains serious and numerous errors in usage, mechanics, and spelling which lead to confusion about meaning.

A paper at score point 1

- only minimally addresses the topic and lacks a discernible idea.

- has only a few simple sentences.

- shows minimal word choice.

- may be incoherent and/or have serious errors in almost every sentence.

A paper is unable to be scored if it is

- illegible.

- unrelated to the topic.

- only a rewording of the prompt.

- written in a foreign language.

- not written at all.

Holistic Guide: Oral Presentation

Directions: Read the descriptions below. Rate the oral presentations in each category.

Outstanding

- **Delivery**—eloquent
- **Rapport with audience**—excellent, showing a flair for public speaking
- **Demeanor**—confident and at ease
- **Content**—well-thought-out, exhibiting humor and creativity

Commendable

- **Delivery**—clear, with appropriate volume and rate of speech
- **Rapport with Audience**—good, using eye contact effectively, showing enthusiasm for subject, and actively involving audience in the presentation
- **Demeanor**—confident
- **Content**—well-organized and of appropriate length, using relevant examples, and exhibiting good grasp of the subject

Acceptable

Includes the elements of a commendable presentation, but one or two are less polished

Needs Work

Includes the elements of a poor presentation, but some are relatively better done

Poor

- **Delivery**—poor, with inappropriate volume or rate of speech
- **Rapport with Audience**—minimal, not establishing effective eye contact, and showing little enthusiasm for subject
- **Demeanor**—nervous to degree that it overshadows everything else
- **Content**—poorly organized and of inappropriate length, using unsuitable examples, including inaccurate information, and showing lack of understanding of subject

Very Poor

Entire presentation is poorly done.

Rubric: Oral Presentation

Directions: Use the rubric scale below to rate each oral presentation.

	Weak	Average	Strong	Score x Weight
Section One Eye contact with audience	rarely	not often	often	_____ x 6 = _____
Section Two Posture	often slouches, sways, turns back on audience, fidgets	sometimes slouches, sways, turns back on audience, fidgets	stands straight, faces audience, movements appropriate to presentation	_____ x 6 = _____
Section Three Voice Projection	words not pronounced clearly and volume too low	words not pronounced clearly and volume too low	words pronounced and heard clearly	_____ x 6 = _____
Section Four Organization	information not presented in a logical, interesting sequence; the audience could not follow	information was interesting but not presented in a logical order	information presented in a logical, interesting sequence which the audience could follow	_____ x 7 = _____
Section Five Visual Aids	two different types of media; information not relevant to outcomes/content; messy; minimal artistic effort	two different types of media; information relevant to outcomes/content; messy; adequate artistic effort	more than two different types of media; information relevant to outcomes/content; very neat; excellent artistic effort	_____ x 5 = _____
Section Six Time	less than 10 minutes	10–14 minutes	15 minutes or more	_____ x 3 = _____
				Total _____ points

Rubric: Product/Performance

Directions: Use this form to evaluate student products and performances. Circle the description that matches your judgment.

	3 Strong	2 Average	1 Weak
Purpose	Statement of purpose is clear; product meets stated purpose.	Statement of purpose is clear; product does an adequate job of meeting stated purpose.	Statement of purpose is not clear; purpose of product is not clear.
Treatment of Subject	Topic is taken seriously and treated thoroughly.	Topic is treated with some respect and is treated acceptably.	Topic is not taken seriously and/or is poorly covered.
Resources Used:	For scope of subject, used variety of resources.	For scope of subject, used limited resources.	For scope of subject, used minimal resources.
Group Project	All members contributed and participated equally.	Not all members were equally involved.	One member did most of the work for the group.
Product, Model, Exhibition	All aspects of product, model, or exhibition represent outstanding work; product makes definite contribution to targeted area.	All aspects of product, model, or exhibition represent acceptable work; most aspects are very good; product shows potential for contribution to targeted area.	Some aspects of this product, model, or exhibition represent good work; the product, if further developed, could contribute to targeted area.
Presentation	Delivered very effectively; time limit observed.	Audience able to understand, despite some problems with delivery; time limit observed.	Audience unable to follow or understand and/or time limit not observed.

Scoring Template for Product/Performance

Directions: Set standards for products and performances. Fill in this scoring template with descriptions of 1, 2, 3 ratings in each category.

	3 Strong	2 Average	1 Weak
Purpose			
Treatment of Subject			
Resources Used: Library People Other			
If Group Project			
Product, Model, Exhibition			
Presentation			

Peer Assessment

Directions: Be an attentive listener as your classmates share their work. Write the titles of the presentations and the names of the presenters on the form below. Use the rubric scale to rate the presentations.

Presentation Titles	Presenters	Rating		
		Purpose	3 2 1	
		Treatment of Subject	3 2 1	
		Resources Used	3 2 1	
		Product/Exhibition	3 2 1	
		Presentation	3 2 1	
		Purpose	3 2 1	
		Treatment of Subject	3 2 1	
		Resources Used	3 2 1	
		Product/Exhibition	3 2 1	
		Presentation	3 2 1	
		Purpose	3 2 1	
		Treatment of Subject	3 2 1	
		Resources Used	3 2 1	
		Product/Exhibition	3 2 1	
		Presentation	3 2 1	

What are the most interesting things you learned?

_____

_____

Rubric Scoring Template

Directions: List criteria in the first column.. Write a brief description in each box (1–3) to indicate the quality of work expected for that rating.

Criteria	1	2	3

Self-Assessment: Product/Performance

Take a few minutes to think about how you went about planning, creating, and sharing your product or performance. Use the sentence starters below to help you write down your thoughts.

1. While developing this product or performance, I spent most of my time on

2. The best ideas I had for this product or performance came from

3. A major problem I encountered while working was

4. I believe that the greatest strength(s) of my product is

5. The major skills I used in developing this product or performance were

6. When the teacher and others judge the quality of my work, I want them to consider

7. Something I will do differently next time I develop a product is

8. The most important concepts learned from developing this product are

Self-Assessment: Product/Performance

What I did	
How I did it	
How I feel about	
Who I worked with	
A highlight for me	
What's next?	

Chapter Four

Process Assessment: Observing Students in Progress

This chapter focuses your attention on observing your students in the process of understanding and communicating rather than on assessing the final results. If you wish, call this "watching minds at work" or "watching thinking in action" or "observing work in progress." In any event, the emphasis here is on understanding the behaviors, strategies, and critical thinking skills your students use as they read, write, communicate, and participate in real-life or simulated problem-solving situations.

The key to process assessment lies in your own observational and conferencing skills. In regular classroom situations, you will have many opportunities to learn more about your students. Note these examples of student processes, strategies, and behaviors:

> reading strategies used to develop interpretations of a text
> behavior during peer review
> evidence of investment in a task
> problem-solving strategies
> collaborative work habits
> processes used while writing an essay
> participating in class discussions
> responses and reactions during conferences
> evolving personal criteria and standards

Characteristics of Process Assessment

1. There are no test items. The assessment requires either observation of students in action or review of work in progress, such as drafts created in the process of writing an essay.

2. Assessment formats vary but often include scales, checklists, and anecdotal records.

3. The evaluator focuses on a student's ability to apply higher thinking skills to a task rather than to recall information or to perform specific skills.

4. The evaluator focuses attention on student processes, behaviors, and strategies rather than on the final results. This isn't to suggest that final results aren't important; they simply aren't the focus of this particular kind of assessment.

Assessing Reading and Writing Behaviors

Because reading and writing occupy so much of your students' time, you can learn a great deal by observing their behaviors and strategies.

1. **Observe your students while they are reading and writing.**
   To keep a record of your students' reading behaviors, use *Teacher Observation: Reading Behavior* and *Holistic Guide: Reading* on pages 42–44. To record students' writing behaviors, use *Teacher Observation: Writing Behavior* on page 45.

2. **Encourage students to keep a reading log.**
   A reading log is a way to record reactions to what is being read. Review your students' logs periodically to check development of active reading strategies.

3. **Keep track of writing conferences with your students.**
   Meeting with your students regularly about their writing experiences will help you understand how they work and will help them refine their writing. Use *Conference Log: Writing* on page 46 to help you keep a record of your writing conferences.

4. **Review drafts students create during the writing process.**
   You will learn about your students' writing strategies and thinking skills when you review drafts they create subsequent to their final draft.

5. **Encourage your students to think about their reading, writing, and other behaviors.**
   You can help your students by encouraging them to think about how they are working. If you haven't already used the reading and writing self-assessment copymasters on pages 11–14, now would be a good time to find out your students' perspectives. Use *Rubric: Process Assessment* on page 47 to share your overall observations about the student as a learner and producer.

Assessing Collaborative Learning

Pay attention to how your students interact with each other and what they learn from one another in peer conferences, classroom discussions, and small groups. For checklists, use *Teacher Observation: Peer Conferences* on page 48, *Teacher Observation: Discussion/Small Group* on page 49, and *Teacher Observation: Collaborative Learning* on page 50. Have them complete *Peer Assessment* on pages 51 and 52 to get their perspective.

Assessing Planning and Organizational Skills

Understanding how students plan and organize work will tell you a great deal about their approach to new tasks. When you meet with them for progress reports, go over their action plans and task sheets. Help them evaluate the effectiveness of their strategies and processes.

Support for Process Assessment in *Language Network*

Language Network provides opportunities for process assessment throughout the program.

- Writing assignments and practice activities within writing and communication chapters provide many opportunities for you to observe your students' strategies, behaviors, and critical thinking skills.

- *Teacher's Guide to Assessment and Portfolio Use* contains many helpful suggestions and copymasters that will help you with process assessment.

Teacher Observation: Reading Behavior

Directions: Use this form as you observe students during the reading process and review their reading logs. Check the behaviors you observed. You may wish to reuse this form several times during the year.

	often	sometimes	seldom
1. Appears to enjoy reading and discussion.			
2. Reads for a purpose.			
3. Appears to be thinking and questioning while reading.			
4. Uses prior knowledge.			
5. Makes connections from text to personal experiences and to other works and ideas.			
6. Makes predictions while reading and tests them.			
7. Explores multiple interpretations of a text.			
8. May revise interpretations when rereading or participating in discussions.			
9. Reviews facts and makes reasonable inferences.			
10. Evaluates text and forms opinions.			
11. Demonstrates understanding of main ideas and issues.			
12. Stays on task and is not easily distracted.			

Comments:

_____

_____

_____

_____

_____

The Holistic Guide describes the kinds of thinking readers can exhibit in the process of making sense of a selection. Do not expect your students to exhibit all of these behaviors. However, the more accomplished readers will show greater depth of understanding and interpretation.

Exceptional 6 points	Perceptive 5 points
• Readers at this level demonstrate a sophisticated, thorough, accurate, and deep understanding of the parts of a work and of how those parts work together as a whole. They show an understanding of nuances and complexities. They draw inferences from subtle cues and plausibly fill in gaps in a narrative. They differentiate between literal and figurative meanings. They attend to and explore ambiguities and contradictions. • They make connections to their own experience and to other works and ideas. They use the text to generate, validate, and otherwise reflect on their ideas. • They explore multiple interpretations and may also revise an earlier interpretation when they reread or participate in group discussion. • They interact with a selection by questioning, disagreeing, agreeing, criticizing, or speculating about ideas and/or text features. They test the validity of arguments through logical analysis and by evaluating the quality and source of evidence.	• Readers at this level demonstrate a thorough, accurate, and deep understanding of the parts of a work and of how those parts work together as a whole. These readers, however, may lack the sophistication and impressive depth of exceptional readers. They show an awareness of nuances and complexities but do not demonstrate the keen insight and understanding of exceptional readers. They draw inferences from subtle cues and plausibly fill in gaps in a narrative, but their observations may not be as acute as those of exceptional readers. These readers differentiate between literal and figurative meanings. They attend to and explore ambiguities and contradictions. • They make connections to their own experience and to other works and ideas. However, the connections may be more predictable than those of exceptional readers. They also use the text to generate, validate, and otherwise reflect on their ideas. • They may explore multiple interpretations and show a willingness to revise an earlier interpretation when they reread or participate in group discussion. • They interact with a selection by questioning, disagreeing, agreeing, criticizing, or speculating about ideas and/or text features. The issues they choose, though, may not be as deep or as significant as those chosen by exceptional readers. They test the validity of arguments through logical analysis and by evaluating the quality and source of evidence.

Thoughtful   4 points

- Readers at this level exhibit a thoughtful understanding of the selection as a whole. They draw inferences from subtle cues and plausibly fill in gaps in a narrative, but their observations may not be as perceptive as those of exceptional and perceptive readers. They attend to figurative as well as literal meaning. These readers are aware of complexities but may be confused by ambiguities.

- They make connections to their own experience and to other works and ideas. They may use the text to generate, validate, and otherwise reflect on their ideas but with less depth than exceptional or perceptive readers.

- These readers do not often explore multiple interpretations. They tend to accept a single interpretation and rarely revise when they reread or participate in group discussion.

- They sometimes challenge or question the issues raised in the selection. They may agree or disagree without explaining why.

Literal   3 points

- Readers at this level demonstrate a very basic and literal, though superficial, understanding of the selection as a whole. They show little awareness of complexities and ambiguities. They may not even respond to a portion of the selection.

- They make few, if any, connections to their own experience or to other works and ideas. Any personal connection to a selection remains on a superficial level.

- They do not explore possible meanings and may even ignore difficult parts of a selection. These readers often refuse to revise or deepen their own interpretation.

- They rarely challenge the issues raised in the selection. If they do, their responses are often expressions of personal frustration or low-level inquiries about literal meaning, such as a definition of a word.

Limited   2 points

- Readers at this level seem unable to grasp the meaning of a selection as a whole. Although they demonstrate a superficial understanding of individual sentences and parts of a text, they do not produce an interpretation that connects those parts or that addresses more than some of the minor points or details of a selection.

- They seldom make connections to their own experience or to other works and ideas. The connections they do make are usually tangential to the main issues of the selection.

- They rarely ask questions or evaluate what they read. They either ignore or become frustrated by difficult parts of a selection.

Minimal   1 point

- Readers at this level show an understanding of isolated words or phrases but do not connect them to gain any accurate or coherent ideas or information.

- These readers may have associations with some part of the selection or an isolated word or phrase, but they fail to connect with the central ideas or characters.

- They do not demonstrate an engagement with the selection or an attempt to construct a meaning.

Teacher Observation: Writing Behavior

Directions: Use this form as you observe students during their writing process. Check the behaviors you observed.

	often	sometimes	seldom
1. Becomes actively involved.			
2. Thinks and plans effectively before writing.			
3. Has a clear purpose.			
4. Exhibits willingness to experiment.			
5. Willingly consults with peers about own writing.			
6. Asks for teacher feedback.			
7. Uses conferencing to refine work.			
8. Successfully revises drafts.			
9. Reviews facts and makes reasonable inferences.			
10. Proofreads and shows care about final product.			
11. Shares finished work with pride.			
12. Evaluates own writing and tries to improve.			

Comments:

_____

_____

_____

_____

_____

_____

Conference Log: Writing

Directions: Use this log to keep track of your writing conferences. Fill in the date, purpose, and people involved. Comment on the outcome of the conference.

Date	Met with	Purpose	Comments

Rubric: Process Assessment

Directions: Circle the appropriate numerical range for student behavior and strategies.

Accomplishments
- meeting worthwhile challenges
- establishing and maintaining purpose
- control of the content and conventions related to the discipline
- awareness of the needs of the audience (organization, detail, interest)
- use of the tools related to the discipline
- creativity

Rating

No Evidence Present						Outstanding
NE	1	2	3	4	5	6

Use of Processes and Strategies
- use of techniques and choices related to the discipline
- use of drafts to discover and shape ideas
- use of conferencing to refine work
- use of revision (reshaping, refocusing, refining)

Rating

No Evidence Present						Outstanding
NE	1	2	3	4	5	6

Development as a Learner
- evidence of investment in the task
- development of sense of self
- evolution of personal criteria and standards
- ability to see strengths and weakness in one's work
- demonstration of risk taking and innovation
- progress from early to late pieces

Rating

No Evidence Present						Outstanding
NE	1	2	3	4	5	6

from Altoona School District

Teacher Observation: Peer Conferences

Directions: Use this form as you observe students during peer conferences. Write the date of the observation and the names of the students observed (up to 8 names). Check the conference behaviors you observed.

Date: _____

	Student names	1.	2.	3.	4.	5.	6.	7.	8.
Peer with Work									
Discusses own work									
Asks for feedback in a focused manner									
Listens to and evaluates feedback									
Uses time for conferencing									
Peer Reviewer									
Listens to peer discuss work									
Offers constructive feedback									
Uses time for conferencing									

Teacher Observation: Discussion/Small Group

Directions: Use this form as you observe students in discussions and small group activities. Write the date of the observation and the name of the student observed.

Class Discussion	Often	Sometimes	Seldom
1. Freely participates in discussion.			
2. Listens carefully and respectfully.			
3. Shares personal experiences and opinions.			
4. Supports own viewpoint with reasons or evidence.			
5. Displays tolerance for different opinions.			
6. Shows confidence in own judgment.			
7. Demonstrates ability to modify thinking.			
Small-Group Activity			
1. Stays on task during group projects.			
2. Cooperates with other group members.			
3. Treats all members of group with respect.			
4. Makes significant contributions to group.			
5. Displays comfort in working with peers.			
6. Completes assigned work.			

Teacher Comments

_____

_____

_____

_____

_____

Teacher Observation: Collaborative Learning

Directions: Use this form as you observe students working collaboratively. Write the name of each group member in the group cell. Note the role each member plays in the group.

Groups	Explains Concepts	Encourages Participation	Checks Understanding	Organizes the Work
①				
②				
③				
④				
⑤				

Peer Assessment: Group Project (midway)

Directions: Use this form to evaluate your group's progress halfway through a group project.

My Name _____   Group Member Name _____

% of Work Done _____   % of Work Done _____

Comments _____   Comments _____

_____   _____

_____   _____

_____   _____

Group Member Name _____   Group Member Name _____

% of Work Done _____   % of Work Done _____

Comments _____   Comments _____

_____   _____

_____   _____

_____   _____

Comments About Your Group (amount of work done by each member, willingness to cooperate, progress toward your goal, and so on):

_____

_____

_____

_____

_____

_____

_____

_____

_____

_____

Peer Assessment: Group Project (final)

Directions: Use this form to evaluate your group's efforts after you have completed your project.

My Name _____   Group Member Name _____

% of Work Done _____   % of Work Done _____

Comments _____   Comments _____

_____   _____

_____   _____

_____   _____

Group Member Name _____   Group Member Name _____

% of Work Done _____   % of Work Done _____

Comments _____   Comments _____

_____   _____

_____   _____

_____   _____

1. What was the most important, idea, or concept you learned?

_____

2. What was your favorite activity? Why?

_____

3. What was your least favorite activity? Why?

_____

4. How well did your group work together? (amount of work done by each member, willingness to cooperate, how the group worked to complete project on time, and so on):

_____

_____

_____

_____

Chapter Five

Portfolio Assessment: Compiling a Collection

A portfolio is a purposeful collection of student work that exhibits overall effort, progress, and achievement over time in one or more areas. In the professional world, portfolios have long been used by artists, writers, photographers, and architects. Portfolios enable students to view the process of development and the products they have created as a whole and to answer the questions:

> What samples show my talents best?
>
> What samples show I have progressed?
>
> What samples show the wide variety of things I can do?

Using portfolios as a form of assessment is an evolving practice that has become increasingly popular in schools as a way to focus on student growth and development. In contrast to traditional forms of assessment, portfolios are ongoing and require student involvement.

Portfolios can do a good job of interweaving instruction and assessment. Because the contents show evidence of progress toward a curricular goal, both teacher and student can more easily see how and what the student is learning.

Characteristics of Portfolios

There are as many ways to work with portfolios as there are teachers and students; however, effective portfolios share these characteristics:

1. A portfolio has a clear purpose, established early in the year and understood by all participating parties.

2. Portfolios are selective—not a catchall for student work.

3. Students must be involved in the selection process.

4. Portfolios must contain evidence of self-assessment and reflection, showing what students know about themselves and their work. These can take the form of letters, notes to the teacher, or other devices that students develop.

5. Portfolios must include a criteria for selecting and judging.

6. Portfolios often are chronological, demonstrating the student's growth and development over time.

7. Portfolios often include a wide array of student work, capturing the depth and breadth of understanding. When considering the contents, be sure to think about product, performance, and process assessments.

Questions to Consider

Following are key points to consider in establishing portfolios. Remember that portfolios are ongoing and evolve throughout the year. Give yourself permission to revisit the decisions you make here as you discover what does and doesn't work for your students.

1. **What is the purpose of the portfolio?**
   Common purposes are
   - to examine the teaching and learning of writing as a process
   - to examine growth over time
   - to assess students' ability to apply learning
   - to focus students' attention on in-depth explorations and area of concentration
   - to help students prepare for job search or college admission

   Portfolio Planning on page 58 can help you think through the planning process.

2. **What are the types of portfolios?**
   Teachers use one or more of these four common types of portfolios.

   ### Working Portfolio
   Purpose: shows a record of a student's work in a particular class
   A working portfolio contains a collection of student products, performances, and test results over a given period of time. The intent is usually to accumulate final results rather than to reflect on the development processes. Often a working portfolio becomes a resource for a showcase portfolio.

   ### Showcase Portfolio or Best Work
   Purpose: shows examples of a student's selected best efforts
   A showcase portfolio contains examples of the student's very best work, including products and performances that go beyond paper and pencil efforts. Often the work meets clearly stated learning objectives and criteria. Student self-reflection is an important aspect of a showcase portfolio. Usually both student and teacher write reflective pieces explaining why they consider the piece(s) the student's best work.

   ### Process Portfolio
   Purpose: shows a student's work in all stages leading to the final result
   In a process portfolio, students keep all information about a work in progress. This collection can include planning documents, all drafts, results of peer and teacher conferences, reflections on stages of the process, and the final product or performance. An excellent vehicle for communication between teacher and student, a process portfolio can become the basis for process assessment. This portfolio can also become a resource for a showcase portfolio.

Cumulative Portfolio or Archival

Purpose: shows a student's best efforts over several years

A cumulative portfolio demonstrates a student's growth and development over an extended period of time. Usually examples are drawn from a showcase portfolio and include a student's reflections on the work. Periodic maintenance is necessary so the collection doesn't become unwieldy.

Use *Portfolio Guide* on page 59 as a sample for letting students know what to include in their portfolios. Use *Content Guidelines* on page 60 to provide a list of possible portfolio samples that might be included. Use *Portfolio Record* on page 61 to make it easy for students to keep track of their selections.

3. **What should the portfolio look like?**
   Portfolios can look as varied as the students who put them together, for example:

hanging files	rubber-banded elastic folders
accordion file folders	five-pocket folders
videotapes	laundry baskets
audiotapes	crates
computer discs	two-pocket folders
manila folders	folder within folder
pizza boxes	drawer in file cabinet
folded paper	whatever works for you

4. **Who decides what goes in the portfolio?**
   Will the portfolio be all student-selected? part student-selected, part prescribed? negotiated by teacher and student? What will be the role of parents and the administration? Regardless of what you decide, do not, under any circumstances, exclude students from participating in the selection process. Use *Reflections* on pages 62–64 to help students reflect on individual pieces for their portfolios. *Four Corners* on page 65, *Reflection Sheet* on page 66, and *Reflection Guide* on page 67 will also help students think about their work. To help students reflect on the final choices, use *Portfolio Selection* on page 68. Use copymasters on pages 73 and 74 to elicit responses from families.

5. **Will there be minimum standards for inclusion of materials?**
   If students are committed to and involved in maintaining their portfolios, you may not need to invoke minimum standards. It's probably more important to emphasize their participation and responsibility than to set exclusionary standards.

6. **What time frame will you operate within?**

At the beginning of the school year, lay out a schedule that includes
> date for getting started
> dates for addition of student work
> class time for the selection process
> class time for conferencing with students

7. **What will be the process for evaluation?**

Be sure to consider evaluation standards and discuss them with students at the beginning so everyone will understand expectations. Determine how often you and your students will evaluate the contents. *Self-Assessment: Portfolio* on pages 69 and 70 will guide students through an evaluation progress. Use *Rubric: Portfolio Evaluation* and *Holistic Guide: Portfolio* on pages 71 and 72 to conduct your own evaluation.

8. **How will you manage and store the portfolios?**

Avoid being the warehouse manager for student portfolios. Student ownership is a big part of portfolio assessment . . . and students should assume responsibility for their materials.

9. **What will happen to the portfolios at the end of the year?**

This is likely to be a school- or districtwide decision. Decide or find out before you start. If any materials are retained from year to year, make sure they are most representative of the student's work.

Possible Work to Include

Work in process
> sample journal entries
> class notes
> rough drafts and revisions
> pages from learning logs
> informal writing
> prewriting examples
> tape recordings or video-
> tapes of group work

Finished work
> representative work
> revised pieces
> research reports
> essay question answers
> history of a work
> examples of diverse kinds
> of writing
> tape recordings or video-
> tapes of dramatic readings
> satisfactory piece
> unsuccessful piece

Reading items
> summaries
> reading record
> responses to reading
> reading log samples
> writings about literature
> book reports
> book reviews

Checklists
> table of contents
> personal spelling lists
> vocabulary lists
> observation charts
> skills mastery charts

Other
> artwork
> oral report outlines
> projects
> out-of-school writing
> poetry
> diagrams

> writing from previous
> years
> pictures of projects
> maps
> tape recordings
> videotapes

analytical items
> reflective pieces
> cover letters
> rationales

Support for Portfolio Assessment in *Language Network*

Language Network provides ample opportunity for portfolio assessment.

- Every chapter gives students an opportunity to write in their portfolio and then revisit their writing.
- Essential Writing chapters and Writing Workshops give students opportunities to polish and perfect the work in their portfolios.
- *Teacher's Guide to Assessment and Portfolio Use* contains many helpful suggestions and copymasters that will help you with portfolio assessment.

Portfolio Planning: Questions to Consider

I. Establish a Purpose

   A. What are the goals for students in my class?

   B. How can these goals be assessed through the use of a portfolio?

   C. Who will be the audience for these portfolios?

II. Determine the type of portfolio

   A. What types of portfolios meet the goals described above?

   B. What is the best way for me to get started?

III. Determine the Contents

   A. What kind of writing will be included?

   B. What other products, projects, performances will be included?

   C. Who will decide which pieces are included?

   D. How will I encourage reflection by the students?

IV. Create Evaluation and Assessment Procedures

   A. How will the portfolios be assessed?

   B. Who will do the assessing?

   C. How will this assessment be incorporated into a grading period or semester grade?

V. Consider Changes

   A. What kinds of changes would you have to make in order to use portfolios in your classroom?

   B. What are some of the problems or concerns you foresee (or have seen) with these changes?

   C. What benefits do you foresee (or have you seen) as a result of using portfolios?

Portfolio Guide

Directions: During this school year, you will develop a writing portfolio by collecting samples of your work. Circle the numbers that indicate what you intend to do.

1. Keep your writing samples in the file or container you prepare.

2. Organize your work in chronological order. Be sure to put a date on every item you put in your portfolio.

3. Include the following items: _____

   _____

   _____

4. Include samples of the different kinds of writing you do.

5. For selected writing samples, include all of the drafts from the first draft to the final draft.

6. Include the types of writing listed on the chart (42). You and your teacher will decide the number of samples for each type.

7. Be selective about what you include. Don't include a sample unless you feel good about it or learned something important from it.

8. For each sample you select, write a sentence or two describing why you included it.

9. At the end of the school year, select your best writing samples. Write a statement for each one, explaining why you included it.

Content Guidelines

Directions: With your teacher, decide what will be included in your portfolio.

Fiction
Include _____ samples from this group.
>   short story
>   character sketch
>   skit
>   scene from a play
>   fantasy
>   science fiction story
>   children's story

_____

Folklore
Include _____ samples from this group.
>   legend
>   tall tale
>   myth
>   fairy tale
>   fable

_____

Humor
Include _____ samples from this group.
>   original jokes
>   original riddles
>   editorial cartoon
>   comic strip

_____

Poetry
Include _____ samples from this group.
>   haiku
>   limerick
>   free verse

_____

Nonfiction
Include _____ samples from this group.
>   autobiography
>   family history
>   character sketch
>   interview
>   magazine article
>   research report

_____

Persuasive Writing
Include _____ samples from this group.
>   editorial
>   news story
>   book/movie review
>   letter to the editor
>   newspaper/magazine advertisement
>   television commercial
>   radio announcement
>   advice column

_____

Work in Progress
Include _____ samples from this group.
>   sample journal entries
>   class notes
>   pages from learning log
>   informal writing
>   prewriting examples
>   brainstorming lists

_____

Other Work
Include _____ samples from this group.
>   artwork
>   diagrams
>   projects or pictures
>   of projects
>   diagrams
>   maps

_____

Portfolio Record

Directions: Use this form to keep a record of the pieces you add to your collection.

Date	Work Added to Portfolio	Notes

Reflections: Perseverance/Improvement

Perseverance

Title of sample _____

I included this sample because it is something I really tried hard to do well. It was difficult for me, but I want you to see that I tried hard to

_____

_____

_____

Comments

- (cut here) -

Improvement

Title of sample _____

I included this sample because I wanted to show you how I have improved at

_____

_____

I used to _____

but now I _____

_____

Comments

Thanks to Sooke School District (#62) in British Columbia

Reflections: Pride/Favorite

Pride

Title of sample _____

I selected this sample because I am really proud of

_____

_____

_____

_____

_____

Comments

· (cut here) ·

Favorite

Title of sample _____

I chose this sample because it is my favorite piece of work done in the last few months. It is my favorite because

_____

_____

_____

_____

_____

Comments

Reflections: Creative/Process

Creative

Title of sample _____

This piece shows my creativity. Please notice the originality of my

_____

_____

_____

_____

_____

Comments

.... (cut here) ....

Process

Title of sample _____

I chose this sample to show you how I develop my ideas before I complete a
final product. I would like you to notice how

_____

_____

_____

_____

Comments

Four Corners

One thing I like about this piece	One thing I need to change
One thing my family and friends would really like about this piece	**One thing my teacher would notice about my writing**

Reflection Sheet

Directions: Use this form to help you reflect on your writing process when you submit a piece for your portfolio.

1. I used _____

   to get ideas for my piece on _____.

2. After prewriting, I decided I would try to focus on

   _____

   _____

3. After I wrote the first draft, I realized that

   _____

   _____

4. When I revised, I made these changes: _____

   _____

   _____

   because _____

   _____

   _____

5. The part I found easiest in the writing of this piece was _____

   _____

   _____

6. The part that gave me the most difficulty was _____

   _____

   _____

7. From writing this piece I learned _____

   _____

   _____

Reflection Guide

Directions: Use this form to help you as you reflect on your portfolio selection.

1. Why did I select this piece for my portfolio?

2. What was important to me about this piece?

3. Where did I get the idea?

4. How much time did I spend on this piece?

5. What processes did I go through in creating this piece?

6. What problems did I encounter?

7. How did I work through the problems?

8. What response did I get from peer reviewers? How did I respond to their suggestions?

9. What kinds of revisions did I make?

10. What have I learned from working on this piece?

11. If I had more time to work on this piece, what else would I do?

12. What are the strengths of this piece?

13. What do I want the evaluator to notice in this piece?

14. What grade have I earned with this piece and why?

Portfolio Selection

Directions: Use this form when you have made final selections for your portfolio.

What I chose   Why I chose it

_____   _____

_____   _____

_____   _____

_____   _____

_____   _____

What I like about my portfolio selection _____

_____

_____

What I don't like about my portfolio selection _____

_____

_____

My work has changed in these ways_____

_____

_____

Choosing pieces for my portfolio has helped me _____

_____

_____

My future goals are _____

_____

_____

Self-Assessment: Portfolio (ongoing)

Directions: Use this form to evaluate your portfolio as you gather material for your collection.

The portfolio pieces that I like best at this point are the following:

_____   _____

_____   _____

They are my favorite pieces because _____

_____

_____

The piece that displays my best writing is _____

because _____

_____

_____

For me, the most difficult part of the writing process is _____

_____

because _____

_____

I would really benefit from help with _____

_____

_____

In the future, the kinds of writing I would like to experiment with are _____

_____

_____

because _____

_____

_____

Self-Assessment: Portfolio (final)

Directions: Use this form when you have completed your portfolio collection.

My favorite pieces in this portfolio are the following:

_____   _____

_____   _____

_____   _____

The kind of writing I enjoy the most is _____

_____

because _____

_____

The work that was most successful for my readers is _____

_____

because _____

_____

The part of my writing that gives me the most trouble is _____

_____

_____

When I compare a recent piece of writing with an older piece, I can see how my writing has

improved. A few things I have learned are _____

_____

_____

My goals for my future writing are _____

_____

_____

_____

_____

Rubric: Portfolio Evaluation

Criteria	3 Strong	2 Average	1 Weak
Versatility	Collection shows student's wide range of interests and abilities.	Collection shows an adequate range of student's interests and abilities.	Collection shows little range of interests and abilities.
Reflections	Reflections are thoughtful. Student reveals strong insights about areas of strengths and improvement, and goals for future.	Reflections are reasonable. Student shows some insights about areas of strength and improvement. Indicates reasonable goals for future.	Reflections show little attention. Insights are lacking about areas of strength and improvement. Lacks goals for the future.
Process	Samples show thoughtful attention to process. Indicate that student has grown from the experience.	Samples show some attention to process. Indicate that student has gained some from the experience.	Samples lack examples of process. Indicate that student has learned little or nothing from the experience.
Problem Solving	Samples indicate that student recognizes own problems or responds to those called to his/her attention through the review process. Shows resourcefulness in solving problems.	Samples indicate that student recognizes some problems or responds to some called to his/her attention through the review process. Shows some resourcefulness in solving problems.	Samples show student's unwillingness or inability to deal with problems. Student does not identify own problems and ignores those called to his/her attention during the review process.
Content, Form, and Mechanics	Student shows careful attention to final product. Content, form, and mechanics show strong control.	Student shows adequate attention to final product. Content, form, and mechanics show growing command.	Student shows little or no attention to final product. Content, form, and mechanics show need for significant improvement.

Holistic Guide: Portfolio

1. How well does the student do with different kinds of writing for different purposes?

2. How does the student deal with/solve problems?

3. How does the student manage process?

4. In what ways and to what extent has the student changed and progressed?

5. What are the student's strengths?

6. What are the student's special talents?

7. In what areas does the student still need help?

8. How well did the student meet his/her goals?

9. How does the student assess him- or herself?

10. In general, how well does the student demonstrate skill mastery in writing?

Parent or Family Response Form

My first impression of this portfolio was _____

_____

_____

As I read the pieces in this portfolio, I was interested to learn _____

_____

_____

After talking over some of the pieces, I began to understand_____

_____

_____

I observed growth in his/her ability to _____

_____

_____

_____

I think he or she could use some help in _____

_____

_____

_____

As I looked through the portfolio, I had the following questions: _____

_____

_____

I would like you to know that _____ has a special interest in

_____

_____

_____

Signature _____

Parent or Family Report Form

_____ , I compliment you on your portfolio.

I especially liked _____

_____

_____

_____

_____

_____

_____

One thing I would like to know more about is _____

_____

_____

_____

_____

_____

_____

One thing I would like you to work on is _____

_____

_____

_____

_____

_____

_____

Signature _____